SAM HAILE

BELLEW PUBLISHING CLEVELAND COUNTY COUNCIL

EDITED BY BARRY HEPTON

PAUL RICE

MARIANNE HAILE

VICTOR MARGRIE

EUGENE DANA

SAM HAILE   POTTER AND PAINTER 1909-1948

First published in Great Britain in 1993 by Bellew
Publishing Company in collaboration with Cleveland
County Council.

Bellew Publishing Company Limited
8 Balham Hill, London, SW12 9EA

Copyright © Cleveland County Council/Paul Rice/
Marianne Haile/Victor Margrie/Eugene Dana

Design by Ken Paskin Bell
Art Editor: Ray Carpenter

Origination and Manufacture by
Excel Graphic Press, Hong Kong

ISBN 1 85725 078 8

CONTENTS

ACKNOWLEDGEMENTS

Cleveland Crafts Centre,
Middlesbrough.

*Amongst its resources is a large
ceramics collection which
comprehensively illustrates the
British Studio Pottery Movement
and a unique collection of
international contemporary
jewellery.*

SAM HAILE is likely to remain an enigmatic figure. Both his life and reputation tend only to be known to the few people who aspire to an in-depth knowledge of fine art or crafts history. The brevity of his creative life and work which offends conservative values, conspires to stop Haile slipping into a neat historical rôle.

This book, and the related exhibition which will tour Britain during the year of publication, is simply an attempt to broaden the awareness of Haile's work and impact. It is intended to set the record for a deeper appraisal on the one hand and a wider popularity on the other.

The project of course, is the sum of contributions from many individuals and agencies. Main amongst these must be the members and officers of Cleveland County Council, in collaboration with Bellew Publishing, supported by gratefully received funding from the Crafts Council.

Paul Rice, who undertook the research as well as the writing of the biographical account, Victor Margrie and Eugene Dana must be thanked for their zeal and unconditional generosity.

The amassing of photographs was a substantial task, made easier by the good will of private collectors and the patient support of colleagues from galleries and museums both in the UK and the States.

Lastly, I must give thanks to Marianne Haile, whose manifest passion to see her husband's life and work celebrated and set into an historical context, has been a major driving force, even if she has not known it.

BH

SAM HAILE understood the nature of art:

… my philosophy of life is therefore simple of statement yet difficult in execution – endeavour to control my environment and to minimize my immediate needs and obsessions, in order to be favourably placed to contact reality through aesthetic experience.

These words, written at the outset of the Second World War, suggest conviction of an extraordinary kind. Sam Haile was a pacifist, painter, potter, writer of considerable perception; full of zest, vital, yet unpredictable. He had great intelligence and a voracious appetite for knowledge. To many students of my generation he gave hope. We recognized him as a maker of pots who dared to embrace the modern movement without need to echo the pastiche orientalism of the Leach ethic. But, in my case at least, this reflected the naivety of youthful judgement as I had seen few actual pots made by either Sam Haile or Bernard Leach. Haile's reputation resided in monochrome reproductions and the acclaim of one or two critics and collectors. The 1951 Memorial Exhibition at the Crafts Centre of Great Britain, then in Hay Hill, London, presented the first concrete evidence for our generation.

Unlike William Staite Murray, his mentor and teacher, Sam Haile was prepared – I believe it became an essential part of his creative life – to theorize about the meaning and practice of art. Murray occasionally ventured into print but the results were often laconic, for example;

Pottery may be considered the connecting link between Sculpture and Painting for it incorporates both.

He rarely explored the problems faced by artists in their struggle to give events both cohesion and substance when working at the margins of experience. Sam Haile's position was very different. The central belief that emerges from his writing is the compelling need to create art, and the necessity to live a life like that makes freedom of expression possible without deviation or compromise.

Freedom for Haile and fellow artists in general could not be achieved through a particular social or political system (though each might play an important part), but to have the strength of commitment to ensure the survival of art. Interference of hostile values, whether from a disapproving state or from internal philosophical strife, could not be tolerated. Despite the inevitable conflicts of conscience, duty to the process of art needed to remain constant. The primary intention was to embrace a condition where art became the determinant centre of existence:

Art is a habit of the practical intellect

From this flowed the means by which the energy within the work of art itself could communicate the profound life of the imagination.

Sam Haile was anxious to formulate critical principles and to evolve a framework within which art activity could be given free play. He was unwilling though, to discuss individual drawings and paintings. They were to remain what they were, revealing their shared meaning without the obscuration of language.

As a member of the British Surrealist group, there is little doubt that Sam Haile thought of himself to be first and foremost a painter; pottery being a secondary concern. Though the pots were regarded as serious labour, they are infused with an apparent sense of ease – relaxed, expressive, cultured and inventive – not bearing the same obsessive compulsion of work seen in other of his works.

I believe the pots are no less important. What clearly emerges is the urgent interrelationship between his writing, painting and making of pots; all dependent on one another but serving different conditions in a manner I do not fully understand, present all at the same time.

Haile's reputation as a potter, in both Britain and the States, rests with comparatively few pots: most bought by perceptive collectors and given to museums. They are not often released for exhibition elsewhere and so are

invariably known through book illustrations and the eyes of others.

It is seldom of value to speculate on what might have been, but the evidence suggests that British ceramics would have taken a radically different course if Haile had not died in 1948; a time of renewed confidence following his awful despair of the later war years. The most eloquent pots constitute a promise to succeeding generations. Seeking totality, the pattern and form engage in a visual dance, where content, allegory and spatial purpose coalesce in unity: 'Chichen Itza' with its reference to ritual sacrifice, reflecting Sam Haile's response to the horrors of war, is a brilliant example. Made during his period of teaching in the USA, it was to become a seminal statement, confirming his powerful influence on the young potters, including Daniel Rhodes, at Alfred and Ann Arbor, Michigan.

Whether Sam Haile would have become such an influential figure in Britain, or Europe generally, is a matter of conjecture but his death denied us even that possibility.

Shepherds Dance, 1937.
Slipware, Dia.32cms. Collection:
Southampton City Art Gallery.

10

SAM HAILE   PAUL RICE

SAM HAILE'S DEATH in 1948, at the age of only thirty-eight, was one of the most tragic losses to British art this century. As a painter, which was how he primarily saw himself, Haile made one of the most interesting, significant and personal contributions to British Surrealism. As a potter, which is how we will primarily remember him, he produced some of the most inventive and challenging work of his time – pots that have changed the direction of modern ceramics. Many agree with Sarah Riddick's description of Haile as:

… arguably the most original artist to work in clay in the first half of the twentieth century.

Haile's creative life effectively spanned about thirteen years, interrupted by personal upheaval and one of the most unsettling periods of modern history. His paintings and pots have endured many misfortunes, but from the small body of work left we can see why he was such a 'fresh wind' and why his short stay in America was so influential.

The majority of artists produce their best work after the age of forty. We can only guess what Haile might have produced if he had lived to reach his prime. It is tantalizing to imagine in what way he might have altered the course of post-war British ceramics or perhaps given greater credence to British Surrealism.

Early and Student Years

Thomas Samuel Haile was born in south London on 8 July 1909. Surprisingly little is known of his childhood. Haile was not close to his family and

OPPOSITE
Sam Haile, 1938.

extremely reticent about discussing the past. His elder sister Eva described both Sam and his childhood as being 'normal'. Haile's father, who managed one of a chain of grocery shops, died when Sam was still in his teens. His mother died of cancer in the early 1930s. No one in the family seems to have had even the slightest artistic bent and it is difficult to know why or when Haile developed the compulsion to draw. By the time he had left school, at the age of sixteen, Haile was drawing regularly and had already made a series of architectural drawings of Norman and Saxon churches in south-east England.

Sam Haile worked by day in a shipping agent's office, and for years attended evening classes at Clapham School of Art and painted and drew long into the night. Eventually, he won a scholarship to the Royal College of Art and entered the painting department in 1931.

His first years were not an enormous success. The head of the RCA, Sir William Rothenstein, believed that 'painting' meant more or less employing the Impressionist style of Walter Sickert. Haile was already much more

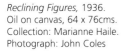

Reclining Figures, 1936.
Oil on canvas, 64 x 76cms.
Collection: Marianne Haile.
Photograph: John Coles

Haile's painting style is still very derivative here.

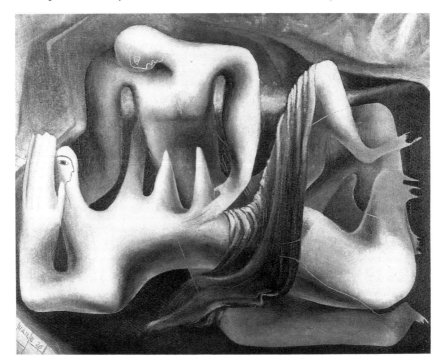

14

interested in contemporary figures such as Picasso, Matisse, Klee and Henry Moore and his work was already showing unorthodox surrealist tendencies. Haile was not of a temperament to play it safe and did not have a great regard for authority. When he was told that if he continued to 'paint like a barbarian' no diploma would be given, he transferred to the pottery department.

This move proved to be fortunate, because the pottery department was run by William Staite Murray, one of the truly great potters of the 1930s and a figure at least as unorthodox as Haile.

Murray and Bernard Leach were the two towering personalities of the British studio pottery movements of the 1920s and 1930s. Murray differed from Leach in that he was interested in pottery as an artistic expression, not in its functional rôle – John Webber described this as Murray's 'enquiries into the very essence of life'. Murray exhibited only at high prices in West End galleries, alongside painters such as Ben Nicholson and Christopher Wood.

As a teacher he was, to say the least, unusual. Murray supposedly said, 'I don't teach, I create an atmosphere.' This was, from most accounts, a considerable understatement. Margaret Rey, one of Murray's most gifted students, told me that the only thing she had ever learnt from Murray was how to sharpen her turning tools. Another, R.J. Washington, described how the only time Murray spoke to him was in order to 'trade' glaze recipes – Murray's least successful for Washington's best.

Maida Vale, 1932.
Wood engraving 12.6 x 10cms.
Collection: Wakefield Art Gallery.

Murray seemed to be removed from his students, yet oddly jealous of their success. He would never attend their exhibitions, never discuss pots with them and refuse to offer criticism.

There are a number of apocryphal stories about Haile's relationship with Murray: Henry Hammond wrote that after Murray had twice refused to comment on his work Haile's persistent request led Murray to 'generously offer' to point with a stick to the pots which he felt should be broken. In Washington's version, when Haile could not get any comment, he finally demanded that Murray at least tell him which ones to keep. Murray walked away, saying, 'Smash all of them.'

Ironically, Henry Hammond, who largely turned towards Leach's style after the war, was the only one of Murray's students who seemed to have a good word about his teacher. But, despite all, Murray produced some

Stoneware vase, 1934. H.25cms.
Private collection.
Photograph: Cleveland County

Haile's radical approach to pottery decoration was already apparent at this early date. This pot belonged to Margaret Rey for over fifty years.

wonderful potters and none better than Haile, who seemed to have an almost instant facility for the medium of clay. Haile must have had some considerable respect for Murray and carried on a correspondence with him for a number of years after his student days.

Haile's pots of the 1930s mostly follow the style of Murray's: thrown stoneware vessel forms, massively heavy with pronounced potting rings, rough sculptured feet and thick lips ('Who would want to kiss a girl with thin lips?' Murray was fond of saying). Haile differed from Murray, however, in two important respects. Where Murray's decoration was

Amazons, 1935. Stoneware,
H.43cms.
Collection: Leicestershire
Museums, Arts and Records
Service.

*The first work of Haile's
to enter a public collection.*

The Long Man, 1938. Slipware, H.76cms.
Collection: Patrick Heron.
Photograph: Bob Berry

One of a series of anthropomorphic pots based on British primitive art.

basically illustrative Haile was interested in using styles then considered radical. The painter Patrick Heron described his work as:

… the first modern pots which bore any relation to contemporary painting … What was new was his decoration: and in this he was the most startling innovator. Ten years and more before Picasso began to design and decorate pots at Vallouris, Haile was creating his essentially contemporary idiom in pot decoration.

Critics have been quick to point out that Heron was more correct in spirit than in fact, but it is undoubtedly true that Haile made a radical departure in decorating style and arguably adapted Picasso's painting style to ceramics rather better than Picasso did himself.

The other great difference in Haile's approach was the way in which he used decoration. In almost all forms of pottery the outside line of the pot, the profile, acts as a visual frame to contain the decoration. Decoration is therefore either conceived as a 360 degree abstract pattern which fits this 'frame' from any angle, or as separate panels that each fit within a frame. On many of these pots Haile would not allow the decoration to fit within the frame. This had the effect of breaking up the two-dimensional illusion. The sculpted foot and undulating edge exaggerated by the potting rings were further unsettling elements. The result is that he created an entirely different way of perceiving the space in a pot, and often gave an unsettled feeling, that a piece could never be comfortably viewed from any single angle. This effect can be seen even in some of his early student works, but becomes strongest in the late 1930s with pots like 'Cretan Feast', 'Orphic Grove' and 'Cerne Abbas Giant'.

Haile spent many long hours in the British Museum, studying not only the Tang and Sung which so inspired Leach and Murray, but also Minoan, Cycladic, English Medieval and slipware, Japanese and pre-dynastic Chinese pots and much primitive art. His knowledge of historical ceramics was wide and his departure from the traditional ways of decorating was obviously more than an intuitive decision.

Haile was given his diploma in 1934 but elected to stay on at the Royal College for another year. He also taught part-time at the Bernard Baron Settlement and Stewart Headlam Institute in London's East End. These commitments meant that he potted only in his spare time, not a situation the mercurial Haile found satisfactory.

The Creative Pre-war Period

In 1935 Haile accepted a full-time teaching post at Leicester College of Art. This proved to be unsatisfactory, since Haile was far too unconventional for Leicester and felt constrained. He did, however, come in contact with the art historian and poet A.C. Sewter, who became one of his staunchest supporters and who persuaded the committee at the City Museum and Art Gallery to purchase 'Amazons', the first work of Haile's to enter a public collection. After a year he returned to London and to part-time teaching at both Hammersmith and Kingston Schools of Art, and also worked at the Royal College.

Margaret Rey had by this time set up a small studio at Raynes Park near Wimbledon and Haile took over part of it for himself. The space was small, but he was able to come and go as he liked, and the small gas kiln was able to fire both stoneware and slipware up to a reasonable size. The few large pots he made were probably fired at the Fulham Pottery, not far from the Stamford Bridge Studio where he lived.

These studios, sandwiched between the railway and the football ground, were extremely run-down and had a leaking skylight. In previous years both Epstein and Gaudier-Brzeska had lived there. Vivian Pitchforth, whose water colours influenced Haile, had a studio in the same block.

Also about this time the Brygos Gallery opened in Bond Street; run by the two contrasting Browne brothers, the gallery had a policy of showing only art 'created by fire', exhibited in velvet-hung alcoves. Rey had made early contact with Ulick Browne, who already had a strong inclination towards Murray's RCA students. Haile (apparently with strong support from Michael Cardew) showed there in 1936 in a mixed show entitled 'Under £10 English Pottery', and had the further offer of a large exhibition in December 1937. Rey was also offered a solo exhibition for spring 1938. Haile had already shown four pots at the Arts and Crafts Exhibition Society's Sixteenth Exhibition, held at Dorland House, Lower Regent Street in 1935, but the Brygos exhibition was altogether more prestigious.

During these two years Haile enjoyed the best conditions he ever found in England. Of course there was virtually no money – he lived on fish and chips, bread and cheese, and enormous quantities of beer, the cheapest foods available in the 1930s. But the working environment was good and he had a large exhibition as a goal towards which to work. Haile was an artist who worked prolifically, almost maniacally well, when in a good state of mind. He had great ease working with clay and could pot quickly. Almost all the work for the Brygos show as well as that eventually shipped to America was made in Rey's studio.

The Brygos exhibition was an unqualified success. Over sixty Haile pots were shown in what was almost a solo exhibition (his friend James Dring also exhibited a much smaller number of 'decorated plates and tiles'). The quality was excellent and the variety was great – from small slipware and stoneware bowls at less than a pound each to larger stoneware pieces at up to fifteen guineas. Also included was 'Cerne Abbas Giant', the first of a series of monumental, anthropomorphic slipware pots based on primitive British art. Critical comment was good, the *New Statesman* described Haile's work as:

Roman Baths, 1936. Stoneware,
Dia.34cms.
Collection: York City Art Gallery.

*One of a number of Haile pots
purchased by Dean Eric Milner-
White, the most important early
collector of British studio pottery.*

20

Cerne Abbas Giant, 1938.
Slipware, H.106cms.
Collection: Robert de Trey.

*This pot, over three feet in height,
was thrown in three sections.
Unfortunately, it was badly
damaged when shipped to
America.*

... the most interesting pottery now being made in this country. Mr Haile finds inspiration for his ornament not in China but in primitive art, like the "Cerne Abbas Giant", and in archaic Greek work. The results are personal, felicitous and often poetical in suggestion.

Ronald Cooper wrote:

... These pots were astounding. The principal pieces were stoneware about fifteen inches high, full-bodied, slightly asymmetrical and more angular than Sung ware. Mythological names such as Dionysus and Aphrodite were given to most pieces and one could imagine that some had been excavated recently in the Mediterranean.

Haile's reputation grew as a result of this work. Sales were an important aspect. Many top collectors purchased pots which were later passed on to public collections: Ernest Marsh purchased two pots for the Contemporary Art Society which were given to the Bristol City Art Gallery and the Royal Albert Memorial Museum in Exeter; Dean Milner White purchased 'Roman Baths' (now in the York City Art Gallery), 'Triumphant Procession' and 'Shepherd's Dance' (now in the Southampton Art Gallery). Hazel King-Farlow, a wealthy American patron, purchased 'Cleopatra' for Leeds, 'Blood Rite' for Wakefield and 'Swan-song' and 'Martian Gleam' which are now both in Liverpool. Charles Laughton, the actor, another major collector in the 1930s, also purchased. Haile was also represented at various group exhibitions in Paris, Toronto and Stockholm at about this time.

The Brygos pots and those made in the following year prove Haile to be a major potter. It is not surprising that they attracted such a positive response. If at times the pots appear a little technically poor, their artistic brilliance more than compensates. If occasionally the forms seem clumsy compared with the decoration, this is more than compensated for by the many times the pots show, in Oliver Watson's words:

... his mastery (one of the greatest we have seen in studio pottery in this country) in integrating decoration with a pot's form and of revealing depths of space in a pot instead of just decorating its surface.

Bernard Leach once said 'the pot is the man'. Although not quite what he meant, anyone who knows potters recognizes that they are terribly like their

Triumphant Procession, 1937. Stoneware, H.42cms. Collection: Southampton City Art Gallery.

Purchased by Milner-White at the Brygos Gallery for twelve guineas.

23

pots. Sam Haile was no exception. His pots convey personal energy, vitality, humour, charm, spontaneity and a challenging and uncompromising nature. They also show a man who was often unconventional, restless, difficult to fit in with and a bit rough around the edges. Most people who knew Haile found him to be a delightful, though sometimes difficult man. His pots are the same.

Haile's world, apart from ceramics, also changed rapidly at this time. On the positive side, in February 1938 he married Marianne de Trey, whom he had met at the Royal College where she trained in the textiles department. He taught her how to make pottery and eventually she became an

Swan Song, 1937. Stoneware, H.45cms.
Collection: National Museums & Galleries on Merseyside.

established potter in her own right. On the negative side, world events were worsening day by day. War raged in both Spain and China, and Hitler's power was rapidly growing. Haile was an avid reader, well informed, with strong political leanings to the left. Marianne Haile once said that if they had not married he probably would have gone to China – although he was a pacifist.

While it is difficult to see this reflected in his pots, Haile's painting, which also matured in the late 1930s, clearly showed the effect of world

Surgical Ward, 1939.
Oil on canvas, 61 x 76cms.
Collection: The Tate Gallery, London.

Sadly, this picture is now in poor condition and rarely seen.

Couple on a ladder, 1941-43. Ink, watercolour and collage, 58 x 46 cms. Private collection. Photograph: courtesy of Marianne Haile.

events. From his works of the early 1930s – very much in the English tradition – Haile's painting had developed in two different directions.

The water-colour landscapes, freely executed and competent, were really a replacement, in a sense, for Haile's potting, and were made when he was away from the potter's wheel on holiday in Dorset or the French Alps. Haile's creative drive and restless energy meant that every day something had to be done and Marianne Haile has written of holidays spent struggling up mountains with an easel. Many of these water colours are lovely, but otherwise perhaps unremarkable given Haile's ability. They were exhibited however, and sold at several places, including the London Gallery.

There were also the surrealist pictures – Haile's important contribution to painting. If the pots and water colours failed to reflect what was happening in the world, this was not so with the paintings and drawings. Haile's artistic nature was somewhat like that of Jekyll and Hyde; by day he would make pots, often covered with light and charming images, by night (Haile slept very little and his drawings were almost always done after his wife had gone to bed) out would come symbolic, often dark, dreamlike images from deep in the unconscious, the natural source material for surrealism. A.C. Sewter described them beautifully:

Their mood is one obsessed by consciousness of pain and suffering, deeply pessimistic, except for the occasional positive notes of sexuality or of the physical activity of dancers. The images of pain are often acutely and disturbingly vivid – heads are distorted, invaded by parasitic plants, decaying or buried; eyes protrude on long stalks; nerves are exposed in tense vegetable systems; feet are suspended from trees or from fragments of parched and fractured earth. Even sexuality, for all its central position in his philosophy, reveals negative and terrifying aspects, as for example in the aggressive and violent sadism of 'The Woodman' or in the saturnine overtones of 'Woman and Puppy'. Yet there is in many of the best examples a poetic sense of wonder and mystery, a sense of revelation of 'deep-guarded secrets', which hint at least at the forces by which man can sustain his agonies and survive them. In 'Strange Fruit of the Stone Sunken One', for instance, the image of torture and destruction is more than offset by that of the female figurine whose vital evocative power survives millennia of burial in archaeological deposits, survives even, maybe, fossilization. The execution is often of the greatest delicacy and elegance of line; the contour often beautiful; the colour even gay and flowerlike. This is not a contradiction of the violence of the imagery, but an expression of the artist's attitude to it.

The form of Haile's paintings changed dramatically in the late 1930s. Pictures like 'Reclining Figures' (1936) and 'Non-payment of Taxes, Congo, Christian Era' (1937) are heavily inspired by Henry Moore. They are sombre in colour with rounded, shaded forms and a strong sense of perspective. By 1939, the perspective is flattened, the colour is brighter, the composition more open, the drawn line is thinner – more nervous and vital

Dream Activity, 1939. Watercolour, 30 x 22cms. Collection: Marianne Haile. Photograph: courtesy of Marianne Haile

Dream imagery was crucial to Haile's surrealist works.

and with a more central importance. Titles like 'Surgical Ward' and 'Brain Operation' are often in contrast with one's first impression of lightness. Perhaps there was an attempt by Haile to bring the two halves of his artistic psyche closer together – as the pots became deeper revealing their interior space, the paintings became more two-dimensional. In 'Man and Falling Woman', one of the last works before his departure from England, he even attempted a painterly equivalent of slip-trailing. It is not hard to visualize this painting's decoration wrapped around one of his pots.

Haile took his painting seriously, and was disappointed by the much easier acceptance of his pottery. At the same time, he was guarded about discussing it – even with his wife – and the work was hardly exhibited in his lifetime. His first major showing was in the Second Surrealist Exhibition at the London Gallery, Cork Street, in 1936, but this was an exhibition

OPPOSITE
Brain Operation, 1939.
Oil on canvas, 24 x 20in.
Collection: Austin/Desmond and Phipps.
Photograph: Colin Mills

Haile made a number of pictures with a similar theme.

Watercolour, 1938.
Collection: Marianne Haile.
Photograph: John Coles

Haile's landscapes are of a very different character to his surrealist pictures.

devoted to objects and it is unlikely that he exhibited any painting (Ian Bennett's assertion that he showed 'Mandated Territories', which is dated 'IV 1938', is incorrect). Even though he joined both the English Surrealist Group and Artists' International Association in 1937, little surrealist work was shown.

Haile did keep extensive notes about his ideas on painting. These are now with Michel Remy, who plans to publish them shortly. They show how deeply Haile thought and felt about painting and contain his rather obscure and sometimes impenetrable ideas about what he called 'the dimension k'. It is highly unlikely, however, that these notes were written with publication in mind. The following excerpt was published in an introduction to a recent retrospective of his paintings:

… The dimension k is intended to express a special mode of existence…the intrinsic value of the rendering is directly proportional to the strength of this factor, or, to the profundity of extension in dimension k. A work of art is therefore an aesthetic object or image extending in the Dimension k … Unfortunately, most people approach the rendering prepared only to receive impressions of the 1st, 2nd or 3rd dimensions. If approached on the plane of the dimension k, the extent to which the rendering exists on this plane (if at all) becomes clear … Dimension k is merely another briefer, and therefore … more convenient way of expressing the amount of human passion (as distinct from individual, often conditioned emotions such as fear, joy, eroticism, etc…) which has accompanied the conception and execution of the rendering in either of the other dimensions.

Aphrodite, 1938. Slipware, Dia.38cms.
Collection: Eugene Dana.
Photograph: Clell Mize

One of the many 'American' pots that were in fact, made in Britain.

Wartime and Life in the United States

The war was coming closer all the time and Haile was determined not to become involved. A decision was made to move to America, and in the summer of 1939, while on holiday in France, the Hailes decided it would be wise not to return to England. Instead, they crossed the border into Switzerland (Marianne had relatives in Lausanne) to seek the visas necessary to enter the USA, leaving Marianne's sister, Juliette de Trey, in charge of packing up Haile's work and shipping it to the States. The Hailes finally reached New York at the end of the year, but Haile's work took another six months to make the journey.

The Hailes arrived in New York, like so many other Europeans at that time, with little money and few tangible prospects. They were fortunate at least to have a place to stay, with Marianne's brother and sister-in-law, who had a flat in Greenwich Village. Bills were just about met, with Marianne undertaking some freelance textile design, and Sam turning to a number of tasks, which he described in a letter to A.C. Sewter as:

… various bum jobs in New York City, e.g. taught in New Hampshire summer camp for the Chosen Race, painted sets for a non-union downtown theatre… designed lampbases for a Hungarian porcelain manufacturer in Perth Amboy NJ, and finally taught on the Lower East Side Jewish, Italian and negro children who accepted me without reservation because they thought my accent was German.

Several of these jobs were not entirely 'bum', as Haile suggests, but they were well below his creative skills. His time at Ford's porcelain works did have a positive side. While it is true that the shapes and materials of the lampbases were dictated to him, there was a certain amount of freedom in the decoration. Most of the lampbases had to be painted with floral and other simple designs, done in a bland and intentionally unchallenging manner, but Haile was allowed to do a small number in his own style. These mark one of the few occasions when a major British artist-potter has been given a chance to collaborate with a commercial pottery.

The teaching job on the Lower East Side was in fact as an instructor at the pottery workshops of the Henry Street Settlement. This allowed Haile to do some real work again, though not under the most ideal conditions.

Cast porcelain lamp base, 1940.
H.30cms.
Collection: Marianne Haile.
Photograph: John Coles

One of the few pieces made at Ford's that Haile decorated totally in his own style.

Tile panel, 1940.
Collection: Marianne Haile.
Photograph: John Coles

*Made at the Henry Street
Settlement. Haile made a number
of larger tile paintings most of
which are now untraceable.*

Perhaps the most important aspect of the job was that it had recently been vacated by Maija Grotell, who had left to take the more prestigious post at Cranbrook Academy of Art. Grotell had arrived from her native Finland a decade earlier and had already established herself as probably the leading influence on American ceramics in the 1930s. The Henry Street Settlement had thus already acquired a certain pedigree, so when Haile's work eventually arrived in the summer of 1940 he was in a potentially good position.

The 'discovery' of T.S. Haile is a truly archetypal story of the American myth of 'overnight success'. Haile had shown his work to Rena Rosenthal, an interior decorator with a good aesthetic eye, who ran a gallery in Madison Avenue. She put on a display of Haile's pots in September of 1940. One pot was placed in the window and was spotted by Dr R.W. Valentiner, director of the Detroit Institute of Arts, who was riding by on a bus. Having found something he recognized as being new to the American art world, he bought a number of pieces both for himself and the Detroit collection.

Word soon spread and the exhibition was followed by shows with the New York Ceramic Society, the New York Designer-Craftsmen Society and an exhibition of drawings at the American-British Art Center. All this attracted the attention of Charles Harder, Director of the New York State College of Ceramics at Alfred University, who invited Haile to teach there. This college, originally created by the English potter Charles Binns, had under Harder become regarded as the pre-eminent establishment for ceramics education in the United States.

Despite being far from New York City, whose high energy appealed to Haile, the tremendous reputation and facilities at Alfred were a strong attraction. Haile's year at Alfred proved to be perhaps the happiest and most creative time of his life, and established him, in the words of Garth Clark, one of the leading historians of American ceramics, as:

… one of the major catalysts of the decade…[an] indelible influence on American pottery.

Robert Richman, director of the Institute of Contemporary Arts in Washington, went further and described Haile as:

… one of the major potters of this century.

Why did Haile have such an enormous impact in America? Robert Richman tried to explain this:

... Obviously meeting art and function at their very foundations, by making for use while transcending it, Haile loved the challenge of working within these confining limitations because he also believed that the greatest in art could be the least. He worked with simple clay bodies, usually stoneware, slipware and simple feldspathic glazes, his colors being mostly iron and copper. If you wish to achieve special techniques or effects in glaze and color, you control the temperature of the kiln. This is the method of the Medieval potters from whom Haile learned and whom Haile liked. To Americans conditioned to ceramic trivia – fishes, gazelles, and earrings – the work of Haile must hit them as a fresh wind. Here is pottery that is not only perfection of form and glazes controlled miraculously, but decorations like those on Etruscan and Greek pots and always the simple statement: 'This is a dish', 'This is a bowl', 'This is a jug'. Haile could throw stoneware to the absolute limit of its yield point and structural strength, achieving thereby a tension of the same essence as sculpture.

The development of modern ceramics in America was many years behind that in England and lacked the dominating presence of Bernard Leach. Part of Haile's impact had simply to do with technique – or, perhaps, one should say, lack of it. At Alfred glazes were made from incredibly complicated recipes, sometimes requiring more than thirty ingredients. While this may have given excellent control and provided wonderful surfaces, it stifled spontaneous creative expression. In England the Zen approach of Bernard Leach and Shoji Hamada had long since eclipsed the more pedantic approach of the chemist-potters like William Howson Taylor and Bernard Moore. Leach and his ideas, however, were still relatively unknown in America. Leach's *A Potter's Book*, the bible of potters everywhere, was first published in 1940, but Leach's influence on American ceramics did not come until his extensive tours in the early 1950s. William Staite Murray had, through his friendship with Hamada, come to ideas similar to those of Leach, at least on the subject of materials. These ideas were naturally passed on to Haile. Haile was a poor technician and a simple and expedient approach was the most suitable for him. His glazes were informal creations of a small number of materials. He replaced perfection with the expressive power of his pots. This was revolutionary in America.

Haile throwing *Three Graces*, 1938.

But it was of course the pots themselves, not just changes in technique, that were the real cause of Haile's impact. As post-war American painting was influenced by incoming European painters, so post-war American ceramics was catalysed by the arrival of European potters. Maija Grotell, Gertrud and Otto Natzler (Austrian followers of Lucie Rie) and Marguerite Wildenhain (from Germany) all had a big impact in America. All used primarily classical, elegant forms with simple decoration and controlled glazes. As Elaine Levin wrote in *The History of American Ceramics*:

…Haile's distorted shapes and casual decoration presented a vision of the vessel in opposition to the precise and more austere forms of Wildenhain and Gertrud Natzler.

This vision was seen more profoundly in the 1950s, when seemingly a whole generation of American potters began to explore similar areas of

LEFT
The Three Graces, 1938. Slipware, H.61cms. Private collection.

This photograph originally appeared in an excellent article in Apollo, *1946.*

RIGHT
Vase, 1939. Stoneware, H.35cms. Collection: University of Michigan Museum of Art.

This pot has been cited as one of the best of Haile's American pots. It was made in England and originally titled either 'Ritual Dance' or 'Equipoise'.

The Stranded Gander, 1940.
Gouache, 46 x 60cms.
Collection: Marianne Haile.
Photograph: courtesy of
 Marianne Haile

The Woodman, 1939.
Watercolour, 32 x 42cms.
Collection: Marianne Haile.
Photograph: courtesy of
Marianne Haile

*One of Haile's most painful and
terrifying images.*

36

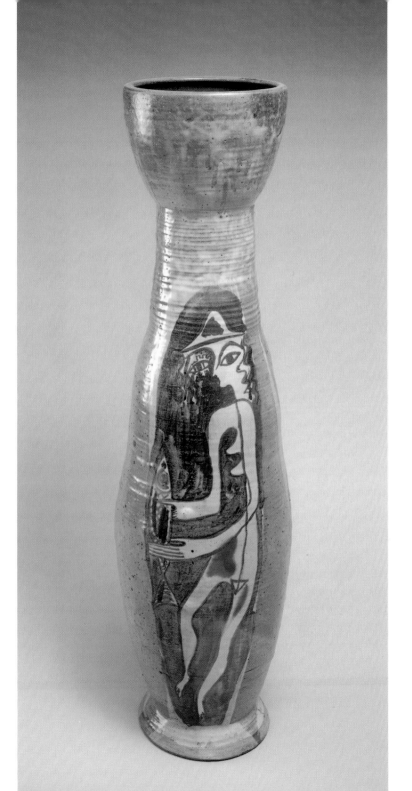

Orpheus, 1941. Stoneware,
H.49cms.
Collection: Everson Museum
of Art, New York.
Photograph: Courtney Frisse

*Haile's prize-winning pot is one of
the most impressive of his
American works.*

Mammoth, 1941. Stoneware.
Collection: Manchester City Art
Galleries.

*This is the only American pot by
T. S.Haile in a British public
collection.*

37

spontaneity, distortion of the vessel form, and the emphasis of art over craft. It is doubtful how much Haile directly influenced potters like Peter Voulkos, Paul Soldner or John Mason, but he certainly pointed the way.

The freedom and good facilities at Alfred meant that Haile was able to produce a wonderful variety of work. At one extreme there was a range of tableware produced by the jigger and jolley method (a moulding technique used for mass-production) decorated using the new technique of raw-glazed silk-screen printing. These pieces are not much better than a humorous and superior kitsch, but Haile was just playing with something new rather than trying to create anything of great merit.

At the other extreme was the large pot 'Orpheus'. Alfred's facilities included massive kilns, and Haile was able to continue the series of huge, anthropomorphic slipware pots begun in 1938. In 1941 'Orpheus' was entered in the large Western Hemisphere Annual Ceramic Exhibition at Syracuse, New York where it was awarded a prize and purchased for the collection by Thomas Watson.

A whole range of superb, large earthenware dishes and bowls with humorous and painterly slip-trailed decoration was also produced. 'Trio' and 'Floral Growth' are two fine examples, while 'Mammoth' was also one of the many good stoneware pots made at Alfred. The potter Daniel Rhodes, who was a student at Alfred in 1941, described Haile as:

… Years ahead of [his] time… creating works of commanding importance both in scale and conception of his superb decoration [which] belonged to the mainstream of Modern Art rather than any debased decorative tradition.

Unfortunately Charles Harder could afford to employ Haile only for one year but, again with the influence of Dr Valentiner, he was offered the post of pottery instructor at the University of Michigan in Ann Arbor, replacing Grover Cole, a student of Glen Lukens. While not nearly as propitious for Haile as Alfred University, this was still a good working environment and resulted in Peter Ruthven organizing a large exhibition of Haile pots in the University's Department of Art and Archaeology. This contained both work from London and Alfred, as well as pots actually made at Ann Arbor. Haile also presented a paper before the American Ceramic Society entitled 'English and American Ceramic Design Problems'.

At Ann Arbor Haile returned to the rough stoneware vases of the type

Plate, 1941. Jiggered and jolleyed. Collection: Marianne Haile. Photograph: John Coles

This whimsical plate was moulded and decorated by raw-glazed silk screen printing.

made shortly before leaving England. Some of these show Haile's increasing interest in Mexican and pre-Colombian art. The finest of these is undoubtedly 'Chichen Itza', one of the most important American pots of the 1940s. This pot, purchased for the Detroit Institute of Arts by Valentiner, is described by A.C. Sewter as:

… an imposing stoneware vase, of severe and noble form. The broad convex curve of its lower half is contrasted by the concavity of the upper part. The title and decoration refer to a late Mayan Sacred Well in Yucatan in which were discovered several layers of remains of sacrificial victims. One of the gods to whom these were sacrificed was Xipe, God of the Flayed Skin. Haile perceived some imaginative relationship between the barbarism of the past and the present war situation, of

Mandated Territories.

Haile 1942.

*which this pot is really an expression. The painting, boldly divided horizontally into
three layers, shows the savage figure of a sacrificial priest, uniting all three zones in
a design of great power. Round the other side totem animals appear above and
below, and the severed arms of sacrificial victims in the dark central band.*

Not only is this pot one of the most important for American ceramics
but, on a more personal note for Haile, marks a real synthesis between the
lightness in spirit of most of his ceramics and the increasing anguish of
many of his drawings.

Exhibition at Ann Arbor, 1943.

Part of the exhibition at the University of Michigan. 'Mammoth', 'Aphrodite' and several other pots can be recognized.

In 'Chichen Itza' and many other Haile pots there is an interesting apparent contradiction. Haile's work is unquestionably modern – the decoration so close to the contemporary art of the time that fifty years later Oliver Watson describes it as having 'a distinctly dated look'. Yet at the same time these pots clearly demonstrate their derivation from (and Haile's respect for) historical ceramics. Leach had made this regard for historical precedents a virtual requirement in Britain. Many American potters in the 1930s and 1940s had not previously considered drawing influence from the great ceramics of other cultures. Even had they done so, it is unlikely they would have resolved this contradiction as successfully as Haile did.

It was almost inevitable that the war would catch up with Haile and in September 1943, not long after the Ann Arbor exhibition, he was inducted into the US Army as a noncombatant. This was not an easy time to be a pacifist. There was widespread support for the war, and pacifists and their families were treated badly.

Return to England

Haile in soldier's uniform shortly before returning to England, 1943.

After six months, Sam Haile was granted a transfer to the British Army and sent to Greenock for further training. Apart from work in the Army Dental Corps – presumably because of the military logic that a potter would be good at making teeth – Haile spent much of his time filing papers and shovelling coal.

This was an extremely unhappy time. He certainly did not have the right mentality for army life, and though not in any physical danger, the war experience was deeply troubling and draining. Haile managed a number of drawings in 1944 and the beginning of 1945, mostly quite anguished works (the 'suspended ones' series of drawings belongs to this time). His increasingly deep depression almost totally destroyed his creativity and he produced little more. A transfer to the Army Educational Corps somewhat improved his position in that at least he could teach, but by this time he was emotionally and spiritually exhausted.

One might look philosophically at this wartime experience as a brief period which added depth his to character. But for Haile it was a dreadful waste, years and energy robbed from an artist whose time was far too short.

Haile was an extremely reckless driver. His release from army life came in late 1945, after he was badly concussed in a motorcycle accident. By this time the war in Europe was over and Marianne had also returned to England. The Hailes moved into a tiny cottage on the Essex and Suffolk border where Sam Haile began work at the brickyard at Bulmer while waiting to be demobbed.

Bulmer Brickyard near Sudbury dates from at least 1450 and may have Roman origins. The yard was bought in 1936 by Laurence Minter, who established a small pottery there for Mary Horrocks. The brick kiln was effective only at low earthenware temperature, and one of the many changes the Hailes made was to build a small coal-fired kiln which would provide the temperatures required for the galena glazes. The pottery became formally known as the 'Bullsmeare Pottery'. Haile designed the seal, which was used in conjunction with his own.

It was a blessing for Haile to get back to working with clay, but most of the early work at Bulmer was more like occupational therapy than creative expression. Much of the domestic ware, mostly designed to be sold in

Watercolour, 1946.
Collection: Marianne Haile.
Photograph: John Coles

Sketch of Bulmer Brickyard.

Bullsmeare pottery bowl, 1945-47.
Collection: Peter Minter.
Photograph: Barry Hepton

Liberty's and Heal's, was uninspired and some of the pots were quirky and fairly dreadful. Only Haile could have made pots as humorous as some of the trophies, and loving cups or decoration as engaging as the stags and bulls that appeared on a number of his pieces.

Haile went back to his roots at Bulmer – using medieval shapes and simple pouring, trailing and dipping techniques of slip decoration. Soon he again produced pots that were wonderful – jugs of almost purely medieval form transformed into surreal objects; slip-painted large bowls and dishes almost as good as the best pieces produced in America. The Victoria & Albert Museum has a number of fine pots from this time, donated by Marianne Haile and James Dring.

Things were slowly getting better for Haile. He was working, reunited with Marianne and often visited by friends like Dring and David Leach (who had been stationed near him at Colchester). Haile could now travel to London, where he often stayed with Robert Savage, a friend who had a frame shop in South Kensington and sold (and collected) a number of Haile's pots.

Five Suspended Ones, 1945.
Ink and watercolour, 36 x 23cms.
Collection: Marianne Haile.
Photograph: courtesy of
Marianne Haile

*Haile's imagery became
increasingly disturbing as the
war progressed.*

Loving Cup, 1947. Slipware,
H.21cms.
Collection: The Board of Trustees
of the Victoria & Albert Museum,
London.

*Made to commemorate the
marriage of his friend James Dring
who bequeathed a number of
Haile's Bulmer pots to the V&A.
The inscription reads: Olive &
James Dring/Drink Be Merry & Marry*

Loving Cup, 1947. Slipware.
Collection: Peter Minter.
Photograph: Barry Hepton

Bullsmeare pottery charger, 1945-47. Collection: Peter Minter. Photograph: Barry Hepton

Another outlet was Paul Alexander in Kensington Church Walk. Paul Alexander was the pseudonym of Alexander Darcovitch, a self-proclaimed 'white Russian' interested in the slipware being produced at that time. Haile's pots, however, perhaps because they were more eccentric and more costly, did not sell as well as those of Henry Hammond, Paul Barron – or indeed those of Haile's wife.

While this was a good recovery period for Haile, things were far from ideal. Slipware was limiting and he did not enjoy making repeat orders. As mercurial as ever, Haile wanted to move on, but was uncertain at this point whether to stay in England or return to America. The US Army paid for him to return to the States in order to get an official release, and Haile took the chance to take stock. Despite being offered a teaching post at the Rhode Island School of Design, Haile stayed only long enough to sell all of his remaining pots before returning to England. This decision seemed vindicated when Bernard Leach told him that his old pottery and house at Dartington Hall were vacant.

Charger, 1946. Slipware. Collection: Holburne Museum and Crafts Study Centre, Bath.

This wonderful pot shows how much Haile was going back to his roots. It is not radically different from some made by Michael Cardew.

Jug, 1947. Slipware, H.33cms.
Collection: The Board of the
Trustees of the Victoria & Albert
Museum, London.

*Using an almost purely medieval
form and a classic slipware
technique Haile has created a
contemporary, almost surreal,
work of art.*

49

At Dartington

Tin-glazed earthenware jug, 1948.
H.20cms.
Collection: The Board of Trustees
of the Victoria & Albert Museum,
London.

*These two pots are of the very few
made at Dartington.*

OPPOSITE
Coffee pot, 1948. Tin-glazed
earthenware.
Collection: Marianne Haile.
Photograph: John Coles

*This animal often appears on
Haile's pots in various guises:
llama/goat/camel.*

The pottery at Dartington Hall had been established in the early 1930s by Leach with the help of Leonard and Dorothy Elmhurst, who had become his patrons. Leach spent a great deal of time there in the late 1930s and wrote most of *A Potter's Book* at Dartington. At one stage plans had been made to transfer the entire Leach Pottery there, but when this idea was eventually dropped Leach turned his attention back to St Ives.

The Hailes moved to Dartington in the early part of 1947. The workshop was extremely run-down and to re-equip and make repairs in a time of post-war austerity was slow and frustrating. Even the simplest materials were extremely difficult to obtain. As a temporary measure they converted Leach's old updraught kiln to oil, but it proved to be uneven in temperature. Haile also built a small electric kiln (which was mostly used by Marianne for tin-glazed ware) and a saltglaze kiln was planned. Haile designed another potter's seal, an acorn (a typical Haile joke; their days at Dartington were punctuated by the loud thud of acorns dropping from a large oak on to the roof). Apart from some slipware and a few experiments in tin glaze, Haile had made few pots at Dartington by the time he died.

Rather than resort to making and selling pots in quantity, Haile had taken a part-time (about one week in two) post with the Rural Industries Bureau as a pottery consultant. He travelled about helping old potteries to redesign for the post-war market. His combination of technical and artistic skills, together with his natural ability to communicate with country craftsmen, made him ideal for this post. This was also quite enjoyable for Haile, partly satisfying his restlessness and bringing in much needed income.

In March 1948, when returning from a trip, Haile drove his converted Jeep into a bus at Poole and was killed.

The Cabin, Dartington.

Leach's house.

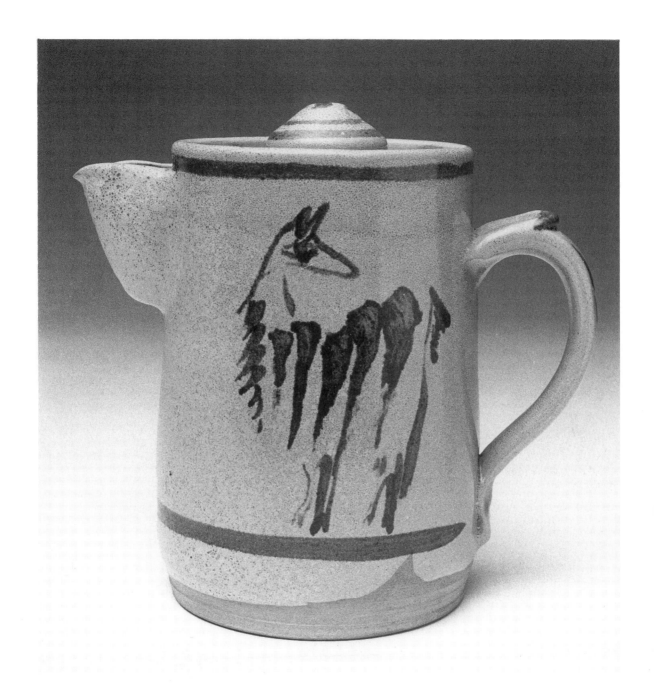

Jug, 1947. Slipware. Collection: Marianne Haile.
Photograph: John Coles
The photograph of this wonderful jug was taken at Dartington.

The Legacy

It seems highly symbolic that his death occurred at the transition between winter and spring. Having survived the devastating years of the war, Haile was coming to what may well have been the best period of his life. He was full of confidence, his creative drive had returned; he had his own house, the part-time job was working well. The pottery was just about functioning and the yearned-for saltglaze kiln only awaited the arrival of bricks. Marianne was pregnant (though it is extremely doubtful that Sam knew) and there was everything to look forward to. Marianne Haile later wrote:

. . . It had seemed as though we were all set to start our new life . . . and yet the tragedy seemed inevitable. In the ten years of our lives together everything had always been at too high a pitch, too exciting, too awful, and though I longed for a steady level period, I couldn't ever quite see it happening.

OPPOSITE:
Large Dish, 1947. Slipware.
Collection: Marianne Haile.
Photograph: John Coles

The tragedy of Haile's early death has been made worse by the misfortunes that have befallen his relatively small output of work. A number of early pieces were lost or destroyed when he left England in 1939. Others failed to survive the car accident when he died (the quality of which can be guessed at from one beautiful slip-decorated charger, rescued and lovingly stuck together by Henry Hammond and presented to the Crafts Study Centre, Bath), while almost half the surviving surrealist paintings and drawings perished in a fire at Dartington in 1957. Many of Haile's best pots, including 'Cerne Abbas Giant', 'Mammoth', 'Shepherd's Family', and 'Long Man' have been broken. 'Avebury Ring', the large tile painting and other works belonging to Robert Savage and Charles Laughton are untraceable and possibly lost for ever.

There is remarkably little left. Only twelve small oils and about fifty water colours, gouaches and drawings are all that remain from his entire surrealist output. A few dozen pots are scattered in museums across England and America. Surprisingly few exist in private hands. Yet, from the small body of work that does remain we can get some idea of why he was so important in his time and we can speculate on what might have happened had he lived.

As a painter it is likely that Haile's work would never really have been totally accepted in England. The British often have somewhat narrow ideas about what is acceptable in contemporary art and Surrealism has never been especially liked. Other artists of the 1940s working in a vaguely similar area – John Banting, Eileen Agar, Ceri Richards, John Tunnard – are still not sufficiently appreciated. It is difficult to imagine that Haile's paintings would be better regarded.

I think it is entirely possible that Haile's ceramics would have changed the course of post-war British studio pottery. There is a widely-held generalization that potters produce their strongest work between the age of forty and sixty. If in this prime of creative life Haile had been able to equal the work of 1937-8 or 1941-2, then there would have been a potent voice against a sweeping tide of Leach followers.

It is almost certain that Haile would have returned to making stoneware. His desire to experiment with saltglaze would undoubtedly have led him back, initially at least, to the painterly, post-Murray pots he produced earlier. If these were exhibited, perhaps Margaret Rey would have felt inspired to make and exhibit more after the war. Perhaps R.J. Washington, far more influenced by Haile than by Murray, would have exhibited the amazing pots he was making but not showing. Perhaps Murray's 1958 exhibition at the Lefevre Gallery would have fallen on more fertile ground. What would have happened had there been a strong 'Murray School' to rival the 'Leach School'? How would this have effected the young potters of the post-war years?

Obviously this is all speculation. Today, when the line between 'art' and 'craft' has largely been blurred, it is almost impossible to imagine how different things were in the 1940s when the dominant voice of Leach's Oriental romanticism stood almost unchallenged. Haile was a pioneer many years before Hans Coper, James Tower, Ruth Duckworth and others who can be credited with dragging studio ceramics into the realm of modern art.

A decade before any of these potters made any real impact, A.C. Sewter wrote:

… Confronted by pottery such as Haile has been making during the last ten years, even a person not normally interested in the crafts is forced to realize that pottery is an art with a range and power of expression not less than that of painting. In his hands, in fact, pottery seems to become at once painting and sculpture … here is an artist whose hands speak eloquent and varied poetry.

Tile, 1940s.
Collection: Marianne Haile.
Photograph: John Coles

55

RECOLLECTIONS   MARIANNE HAILE

BEING ASKED, suddenly, to write about Sam is a tough proposition – not because my memory is blurred after thirty years or forty years but because I want to say something which is relevant for today to those people to whom thirty years might just as well be three hundred. Because so much has happened in that time (and not the least in the ceramic field) it seems important to record personal experiences and reactions rather than to assess them historically.

One thinks first of Sam's enormous vitality, his Rabelaisian sense of humour and his contempt for ordinary middle-class attitudes. He was a man of great intelligence and had a voracious appetite for knowledge. But he was unpredictable, and life with him – though never dull – was difficult. Not only Rabelais, but Breughel too was a favourite of his, and his moods would change from the boisterousness of the one to the torment of the other – without warning – and there would be periods of despair.

But he changed my life: he opened my eyes and ears, breaking down the barriers and clearing out the rubbish. He gave me a bad time, but a good time too, and it was always unexpected. At a time when practically nobody else (apart from Bernard Shaw and Augustus John) had a beard, Sam shaved off his own beard one night, and I woke up beside a complete stranger. He, the most anti-violent of people, once had a fight in a New York bus because he thought a man was fresh with me.

He was a Londoner, and proud to be related to the 'pearly kings' – the élite of the costermongers of Victorian days. He left school at sixteen and worked for several years in a shipping office, attending evening art classes and painting half the night. Eventually he won a scholarship to the Royal College of Art where, a couple of years later, I met him.

OPPOSITE
Nymphs and Satyr, 1939.
Stoneware, H.40cms.
Collection: John Keatley Trust.
Photograph: Cleveland County

Sam Haile, 1936.

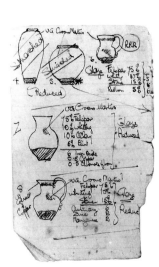

Page of notebook kept by Sam Haile while at the Royal College of Art.

It is difficult today to realize what a gap could exist between the avant-garde of that day and the 'Art School' establishment, between Picasso, Matisse, Klee and Miro and the conventional academic style that Sam was expected to use. Being a rebel, he objected; but fortunately for him, he one day found himself in the pottery department and suddenly realized his opportunity to qualify for his diploma without betraying his convictions or boring himself to death. Fortunately too, W. Staite Murray – himself way ahead in attitude compared with the painters and sculptors – was in charge, and he allowed Sam to work as he liked. The old Morris Arts and Crafts Movement had been followed by 'Art Nouveau' and a dash of Cubism, but by 1930 the Bauhaus was much discussed and there was a return to natural materials and an emphasis on texture, form and function. (As a student in the textile department, I was busy with batik, tie and dye, wood blocks, spinning and vegetable dyes). For potters, a magnificent Chinese exhibition, with its emphasis on the early T'ang and Sung periods, was a turning point. Almost simultaneously Bernard Leach was writing, Michael Cardew had revived the Old Pottery at Winchcombe and the whole English slipware tradition was waiting to be rediscovered.

For Sam, with his insatiable appetite, there was much more – early Greece, the Near East, the whole of Africa – pots, masks, bronzes and carvings. (These were of course available in the museums, but many of them were sitting in dusty ethnological departments, waiting for someone to notice them.) Sam was much influenced by publications such as *Cahiers d'Art* and *Minotaure*, with their juxtapositions of the newest ideas in the arts, music and literature with the very oldest – those of Picasso with those of Palaeolithic man, those of Gregorian chants with those of Poulenc. Surrealism especially interested him, with its ferocious attack on bourgeois ethics, and he joined the English group of surrealists in 1936.

Sam was very politically and socially conscious – aware of the fantastic richness of life, but also of the terrible difference between affluence and poverty and between surface and reality. By about 1937 there was a strong undercurrent of feeling that the world was going badly. Nowadays nobody is surprised if artists and intellectuals take an active stand on political issues, but forty-five or so years ago this was unheard-of. There was not only the obvious menace of Hitler, but there was a revolution in Spain and another in China. (Sam did not want to join the International Brigade, but he would have gone to China had he not married me.) The Left Book Club, May Day marches, demonstrations against Franco – all were very much a part of our lives, but they were interspersed with much work, Mozart or Stravinsky at the Queen's Hall and even brief visits to Paris to hear Wanda Landwska play her harpsichord or to see special exhibitions.

I didn't attempt to keep up, especially on the intellectual side. Sam was reading Eliot and Joyce – he bought chapters of 'Work in Progress' (one at a time) before it was published as *Finnegans Wake* – and he was reading the French surrealists – Eluard and Breton, then Spengler and Pareto, Coomaraswamy and Maritain, while I was still plodding along with Huxley and a bit of Freud, trying to understand Virginia Woolf and pretending not to be shocked by Henry Miller.

Soon after leaving the college, Sam obtained a part-time teaching position in London and he shared a pottery studio with Margaret Rey who had a small, gas-fired kiln which they used for both stoneware and earthenware. The space was tiny, but all Sam's best pots (including those later exhibited in New York in 1940) were made in this brief period between 1937-39. He did also have some success in exhibiting both paintings and drawings. Sam was painting hard in his spare time, and we had two long summer holidays in the French Alps where he made numerous water-colour drawings of the mountains. At that time the pots seemed to have nothing in common with the paintings, or the paintings with the drawings, but they were all important to him.

It became obvious early in 1939 that war would come, and we decided to emigrate to the United States (Sam being, at that time, a conscientious objector). We were fortunate in being able to live with my brother and sister-in-law in New York City until Sam found a job teaching in the Henry Street Settlement on the Lower East Side – a pretty rough area in those days, where few people seemed to speak English, let alone understand a Limey's accent.

Eventually the pots from England turned up and were exhibited on Madison Avenue, and this changed everything for us. Charles Harder, then the Design Professor at Alfred University, was so enthusiastic that he managed to secure some teaching for Sam for the following year, even though no job was really available. Thanks to Charles we had a splendid year – Sam potting and teaching, and I allowed to use the premises as I

Invitation to the 1937 exhibition at the *Brygos Gallery*.

Strange fruit of the stone sunken one.

H 2/6/44

wished. Dan Rhodes was also there that year getting his master's degree and the Misses Fosdick and Nelson were both still teaching.

I think Sam's outlook came as a breath of fresh air. At Alfred University the pots had beautiful glazes but were otherwise dull; Sam's pots were the opposite. He was never a good technician, and his glazes were so simple that they were laughable to the chemistry department – but they worked. He was versatile and ready to try anything. The department was small but had good facilities for experiment, and we both did some salting and some raw-glazed silk-screen printing – a new technique then and one that suited Sam's ability as a draughtsman.

The following year Sam taught in Ann Arbor, and there was a good exhibition organized by Peter Ruthven.

The war finally caught up with us, as we knew it must, and Sam joined the US Army as a noncombatant. His feelings about conscientious objection had modified somewhat, and he did not wish me to be subjected to the ostracism and general unpleasantness suffered at the time by the wives of conscientious objectors. He was assigned to the Dental Corps and was on his way to becoming a mechanic (I have a tiny silver skull which he made for me instead of casting teeth) when he was transferred to the British Army. He was interested to see England again after four years' absence, but the exchange was not a happy one. We had both learned to enjoy America, and he found army life in England to be disagreeable physically, and to be emotionally and intellectually depressing. Eventually, after a dreary period as an office clerk, Sam managed to get into the Education Corps and was able to teach again. He found nearby (at Bulmer in Suffolk) a brickyard with a pottery attached and, the European war being over by that time, I was able to return to England to work there and to be near him while he waited patiently for demobbing – the magic moment of freedom which came nearly a year later. We stayed at Bulmer until the end of 1946, making slipware which was first fired in the brick kiln and then in a small coal-fired saggar kiln which Sam built.

As for so many others, army life was a frustrating experience for Sam. His creative powers had been blocked at a critical period – in his mid-thirties, just when they should have been at their height, and he found it difficult to adapt. In 1944 he wrote a long article (closely argued and full of footnotes) for a periodical about the artist and war. In it he stated that he

Extract from 1944 article.

"It is not for himself that [the artist] seeks to warn his contemporaries when he sees their spiritual gropings. Provided he can keep enough freedom to continue his craft, it matters little to him if it is the people's wish to cut each other's throats. Naturally he ignores all calls of duty toward such abstractions as Flag, Fatherland and Freedom, for he has two duties only, or rather two aspects of the same duty which is to art, its two facets being the artistic virtue and the propaganda of the message... By propaganda in this context is meant not a didactic, calculated effort to make converts, as in advertising and commercial art or in Ministries of Information and Propaganda, but the inevitable propaganda released by the explosion of revealing through the work of art the profound life of the imagination."

believed that the duty of an artist was not to be concerned with patriotism, or with killing or being killed, but to be concerned with keeping open the channel for the 'habit' of art and the channel within himself. Sam had continued to draw when he could (which was seldom), but it was a long time before he regained confidence. He felt that he had shot his bolt and that younger men were getting ahead, and his negative feelings were greatly increased when he suffered a serious concussion from a motorcycle accident from which he never, perhaps, fully recovered. He decided that the only thing to do was to return to the roots of simple slipware, and soon he was turning out a splendid series of jugs, rather medieval in form, which had all the old vigour about them.

It seemed the right moment to move somewhere with more space, and when Bernard Leach told us that his old pottery and house at Dartington Hall were now vacant, we jumped at the chance and came here early in 1947.

The war had deeply affected every aspect of life. Not only did the rationing of food continue for a long time, but it was hard to obtain the simplest materials for building – wood, nails, nuts, bolts of the right size and so on – and we needed new kilns, wheels, everything. Not wishing to be a repetition thrower, Sam worked part-time for the Rural Industries Bureau as a pottery consultant, helping old potteries to redesign for the present market – a job he enjoyed but which took him away about one week in two.

We bought a rather crazy-looking converted Jeep, and Sam was a terrifying driver. He was hurrying home from London (had sent me a special loving note with one of his usual funny drawings, to say he'd be home a day early) when he hit a bus; ironically, it was his right of way – the accident therefore not strictly his fault – but this was in the days before traffic lights and roundabouts. It had seemed as though we were all set to start our new life: the house and pottery were there, I was pregnant, he was well and full of confidence. And yet the tragedy seemed inevitable. In ten years of our lives together everything had always been at too high a pitch, too exciting, too awful, and though I longed for a steady level period, I couldn't ever quite see it happening.

One must accept, I fully believe, that everyone has a 'role to fulfil', and that the rights and the wrongs are all part of it, so that if a man leaves the world enriched in any way, he has done well.

Marianne Haile, 1978.

Postscript

I wrote this over ten years ago, and it still seems substantially right. Rather than alter anything I would only add a postscript.

More than forty years on, I still miss him. How I would enjoy discussing everything from 'crop circles' to Chaos Theory (but then again, could he have come to terms with the ecological and political mess that we face?) I remember best the bright flame, but the dark shadows were very powerful. I know that he burnt himself out. Had he lived longer I like to think he might have learnt to reconcile the two opposites; for what was it all about if not about the Tao? I found yesterday a quotation from Rumi, a thirteenth-century Sufi poet, and it seems to represent the drive behind Sam; it simply says:

...I am the flute; thine is the music.

A MAN of thirty-five years, of moderate height, sturdily built. The face was open with ruddy cheeks and very blue eyes; a high forehead was open with straight, blond hair. The man had wit, ready and often quite ribald ('tighter than a fish's ass').

He was not overtly talkative with casual friends, but with his students, comments and directions were given precisely, generously and pleasantly. In the early 1940s at the University of Michigan, he formed a friendship with Professor James Marshall Plumer, Chairman of the Far Eastern section who, in 1935, had discovered a kiln site in northern Fukien, and was able to 'document the provenance of most of the true "Chien" bowls in our present-day collections'. In his overview of Chinese art, whether it be painting, ceramics or workings in metal, Plumer's axiom, quite his own, was 'never more than convention, never less than symbol'. It would appear that Sam Haile regarded this implicitly, for the form of his pots, arising naturally on the wheel, was tradition-conventional, and his decoration, never totally naturalistic, became pure symbol, as evident in his restructuring of human anatomy.

Sam had already started to teach himself Chinese, and Plumer was enormously helpful with Sam's written Chinese. A batch of Sam's home-made wine was labelled in Chinese, although Marianne was not about to offer it to anyone who might know the language; there was no telling what the label might have said.

Professor Plumer defined decoration as 'suitable embellishment', surely an unequivocal statement. Sam was a painter before becoming a potter. However, a painter's vision does not always guarantee suitability on a pot. Sam respected those sections of a pot – neck, shoulders, belly and foot – as

OPPOSITE
Jug, 1938. Slipware, H.30cms.
Collection: Eugene Dana.
Photograph: Peter Lee

This is catalogued in America as being titled 'Three Horses' and made 1940-2. In fact it is one of a series of similar (untitled) jugs made at Margaret Rey's London studio and sent to America.

melding structurally and harmoniously into a whole, and whatever application of slip, brushed or trailed, had to 'fit' into and upon those areas; it had to 'belong'.

The pitcher was still on the wheel, undecorated as the handle had yet to be applied. The clay was pulled to the proportion of neck and body, one end secured at the neck, the other placed on to the body. Then, with blinking swiftness, in order to secure handle to pot, two fingers rode over this end, cutting so forcefully into the clay body that the joining was almost severed. Jim Plumer's dictum that 'a pot is to be held with two hands' also implies the admonishment 'and rarely by the handle'. The pot became the 'Horse Pitcher', white slip trailed into and upon. Two very male equines pursuing a frightened mare. Around and around. And still pursuing fifty years later.

Illinois, September 1992

And a Man Stepped out of the crowd who reluctantly admitted he was a gas-inspector, 1941-3. Gouache, 44 x 58cms. Collection: Andrew Murray. Photograph: courtesy of Marianne Haile

One of Haile's most complete expressions.

Plate, 7 x 37.1cms.
Collection: The University of
Michigan Museum of Art, gift
of Miss Catherine B. Heller.

CHRONOLOGY

1909
Born in London

1923-31
Leaves school at fifteen.
Works for several years in a shipping office.
Attends evening classes at Clapham School of Art, London

1931-34
Wins scholarship to study painting at the Royal College of Art.
Switches to Pottery Department run by William Staite Murray

1935
Full-time pottery instructor in Department of Industrial Design, Leicester College of Art.
Exhibits pots at 16th Exhibition of Arts and Crafts Society, Dorland House, London

1936
Returns to London to teach part time at Kingston and Hammersmith Schools of Art

1937
Exhibits over sixty pots at Brygos Gallery, New Bond Street, London.
Joins Artists International Association and English Surrealist Group

1938
Marries Marianne de Trey. Teaches her to make pottery.
Work included in exhibitions in Paris, Stockholm, Toronto and London

1939
Leaves England for summer in Switzerland.
Moves to United States

1940
'Various bum jobs', including teaching crafts at a summer camp, painting theatre sets and teaching children from Lower East Side settlement houses in New York.
Designs and decorates lamp bases for a Hungarian porcelain manufacturer in Perth Amboy, New Jersey.
Exhibits pots in Rena Rosenthal's Gallery on Madison Avenue and discovered by W.R. Valentier

1941
Exhibits pots with the New York Ceramic Society and New York Designer-Craftsman Society.
Exhibits drawings at the American-British Art Centre.
Begins to teach and study at New York State College of Ceramics, Alfred University.
Exhibits at Western Hemisphere Annual Ceramic Exhibition, Syracuse, NY. Awarded prize for the stoneware pot 'Orpheus', now in the Everson Collection

1942
Appointed pottery instructor at College of Architecture, University of Michigan, Ann Arbor

1943
Has large exhibition of pottery in university's Department of Art and Archaeology.
Inducted into US Army

1944
Transferred to British Army and sent to Britain. Becomes sergeant-instructor in Army Educational Corps

1945
Concussed in motor cycle accident and discharged from service.
Makes pottery at Bulmer's brickyard near Sudbury, Suffolk

1946
Appointed pottery consultant to Rural Industries Bureau.
Exhibits slipware at Paul Alexander's shop in Kensington, London

1947
Moves to Shinner's Bridge, Dartington, Devon.
Exhibits Surrealist drawings at the London Gallery

1948
Begins experimenting with salt glaze and stoneware. Killed in car accident at Poole, Dorset – March 1948
Memorial exhibitions at Southampton Art Gallery and Institute of Contemporary Arts, Washington DC

1951
Memorial exhibition at the Crafts Centre, London

1967
Large touring exhibition of surrealist drawings and paintings organised by the Manchester Institute of Contemporary Arts

1971-91
Included in numerous group exhibitions

1987
Exhibition of paintings and drawings at Birch and Conran, London

Works in Public Collections in the UK and USA

Many of the works referred to in this book can be found in the following museums:

Bath
Holburne Museum and Crafts Study Centre

Bradford
Cartwright Hall

Bristol
Bristol City Museum and Art Gallery

Cambridge
Fitzwilliam Museum

Exeter
Royal Albert Memorial Museum

Leeds
Lotherton Hall, Leeds City Art Galleries
Leeds City Art Gallery

Leicester
Leicestershire Museum and Art Gallery

Liverpool
Liverpool Museum, National Museums and Galleries on Merseyside

London
Tate Gallery
The Victoria and Albert Museum

Manchester
Manchester City Art Galleries
Whitworth Art Gallery

Paisley
Paisley Museum and Art Galleries

Royston, Hertfordshire
Royston and District Museum

Southampton
Southampton City Art Gallery

Stoke-on-Trent
City Museum and Art Gallery

Wakefield
Wakefield Art Gallery

York
York City Art Gallery

Detroit
Detroit Institute of Design

New York
Everson Museum of Art, Syracuse

Michigan
The University of Michigan Museum of Art, Ann Arbor

BIBLIOGRAPHY

In chronological order:

T.S. Haile, Potter and Painter
*A.C. Sewter, Apollo, December
1946 and (edited) Pottery in Glass,
March 1947*

The Modern Potter
R.G. Cooper; Tiranti, London, 1947

The Art of Living
*Robert Richman; Architectural
Forum, March 1949*

T.S. Haile, Ceramist
Craft Horizons, Summer 1949

T.S. Haile
*A.C. Sewter; catalogue for memorial
exhibition at Crafts Centre in
London, 1951*

Round the London Art Galleries
*Patrick Heron; the Listener
September 1951*

The Work of the Modern Potter in
England
*George Wingfield-Digby; John
Murray, London, 1952*

Artist-Potters in England
*Muriel Rose; Faber & Faber, London,
1955*

The Surrealist Paintings and
Drawings of Sam Haile
*A.C. Sewter; catalogue for exhibition
at Manchester City Art
Gallery, 1967*

People Are Not Afraid of These
Things Now
*Marianne Haile; Dartington Hall
News, 7 March 1969*

Sam Haile
*Garth Clark and Marianne Haile;
Studio Potter, 1977*

A Century of Ceramics in the United
States
*Garth Clark and Margie Hughto;
E.P.Dutton, New York, 1979*

British 20th Century Studio Ceramics
*Ian Bennett; catalogue for exhibition
at the Christopher Wood
Gallery, 1980*

William Staite Murray
*Malcolm Haslam; Crafts
Council/Cleveland County Council,
1984*

Sam Haile
Michel Remy, Oliver Watson and

*Marianne Haile; catalogue for
exhibition at Birch & Conran, 1987*
American Ceramics
*Garth Clark; Booth-Clibborn
Editions, London, 1987*

Sam Haile - Painter and Potter
*Marianne Haile; Ceramic Review
No.107, 1987*

The History of American Ceramics
*Elaine Levin; Harry N. Abrams,
New York, 1988*

American Studio Ceramics 1920-
1950
*Catalogue for exhibition, University
Art Museum, Minnesota, 1989*

British Studio Ceramics in the 20th
Century
*Paul Rice and C.Gowing; Barrie &
Jenkins, London, 1989*

Pioneer Studio Pottery; The Milner-
White Collection
*Sarah Riddick; Lund Humphries,
London, 1990*

British Studio Pottery
*Oliver Watson; Phaidon-Christies,
Oxford, 1990*